To Charlotte, my daughter

A little girl in tears
In a city in the rain . . .
—CLAUDE NOUGARO

La Petite

I'm twelve years old, and this evening, I'll be dead.

This morning I emptied the bottles of sleeping pills and all the other medicines Maman stores on the top shelf of the cabinet in the bathroom to keep them out of reach. It took me five big glasses of water to swallow everything. Next, I ate some bread and butter, drank my orange juice, and set out for school.

I said nothing to anyone. I am neither depressed nor overexcited. I feel serene, the way one is when doing what one really wants to do. And what I want to do is disappear.

~~~~~~

It's five minutes past nine. I'm in study hall. My classes don't start until ten, but I decided to leave the house as early as possible. I don't know when it will happen. Probably by midday. Will I fall off my chair, or simply go to sleep? I don't feel tired. By tomorrow everyone will have forgotten that I spent my last study hall on the bench in the fourth row on the left, two tables from the window.

I see latecomers crossing the school grounds at a run, even though it's absolutely forbidden to walk on the grass. I never dared. Too late now.

The students around me are diligently doing their homework. I, too, am concentrating on the paper in front of me. But I'm not working. I am writing.

I ought to have thrown out all my notebooks. If someone discovers them, will I ever be in trouble! No, that's silly of me. I won't be here anymore. Nothing more will happen to me. As the nurse says at the end of a blood draw, when she loosens the tourniquet: it will soon be over.

I got caught in the middle of science class. I'd dozed off, facedown in the crook of my arm. Even though I'd carefully stacked some books in front of me, that old bag Gauthier finally noticed that I'd fallen asleep.

Amazingly, her voice was calm, almost gentle, when she told the girl next to me to escort me to the infirmary.

Poor Caroline, blushing with embarrassment, was scandalized.

"You're crazy! She could have stuck you with detention for the whole afternoon!"

After glancing at me, she lightens up a little.

"Actually, the way you look, no one would think of yelling at you. Your face is so white!"

My being sent to the infirmary is really annoying. It's only ten past eleven. I certainly don't want anyone calling home; Maman would come get me and nag me with questions. Which isn't at all what I'd planned. What I want is for people to let me sleep— and die in peace.

Luckily, on Wednesdays there's only one nurse on duty, and after Caroline knocks and opens the frosted-glass door, we see Mlle. Jamin from the back, crouching as she wipes a coarse floor cloth over the ocher tiles, where a sixth-grader has just thrown up her breakfast.

Still with her back to us, Mlle. Jamin asks me about my symptoms. I invent a sleepless night for myself, a migraine, I'm simply feeling dizzy, that's all. No, I don't think my parents are home this morning. Yes, when I get home, if I don't feel better, I will call the doctor.

Believing me, because she has no reason not to, she gives me a scratchy rectangular pillow, an itchy brown blanket, a few drops of soothing mint extract on a sugar cube in a little spoon, and decides that it's more urgent to reach the parents of the little six-grade girl than to take care of me.

Thank you, mademoiselle: forget me, that's all I ask.

Back to sleep I go.

The door of the infirmary swings open on my mother's square glasses and beige silk dress, and I can tell from her strained look that Maman is still furious with me. After our argument yesterday, she's not about to cut me any slack. That shrillness in her voice gives her away, and the stiff way she moves. She's here, but distant; efficient, but noticeably curt with me.

She takes my arm brusquely. No doubt she thinks she's on top of the situation. Ordinarily, I detest these black days when she won't look me in the eye, when my questions meet only with silence, when my pitiful peace offerings leave her cold. Today, though,

I couldn't care less. Oh, if she only knew! But, that's precisely it: she mustn't.

I let her drag me to the car. I don't even switch on the radio right away as I usually do, but she appears not to notice. Too busy working her way through the traffic jam.

My legs are numb and my mind is woozy. Between the sleeping pills and my determination not to nod off, I feel like the classic alcoholic in the movies who swears he's fine right after he's downed one drink too many.

I have to carry this off. And hang on for another few hours. My worst fear is that they'll pump my stomach and the next day say, "She lost her head for a moment but that's over now, let's not discuss it anymore," when that's all everyone will think about from then on.

I did not send out a cry for help, I raised no alarm, sent up no flares. I don't want people to save me and then ask themselves why I did it. It's been too late for that for a long time now.

Fortunately, Maman doesn't seem worried. She's still too angry with me. She must think that feeling faint is the least you can do after getting on your mother's nerves so much. Maybe she even sees it as the sign of a guilty conscience. Well, let her.

I open the car window, but the May breeze is too mild to give me the bracing shock I'd hoped for. It's only a short ride home from school, but I'm already drowsy. Getting out of the car, I can hardly feel my legs. My book bag is way too heavy. Feeling Maman's eyes on me, I try to walk to the front door of our building as normally as possible.

Even before putting down her purse, the first thing she does when we get home is call the doctor who's been taking care of us for so long that Maman will risk disturbing him at lunchtime. I hear her telephoning him out in the hall. Please let her get a busy signal, let the phone be off the hook so he can eat undisturbed! No, too bad, she's talking. Not for long. She hangs up, then joins me in my room, nervous and irritated. She'd just missed him, and had spoken with his wife. He's out on an emergency call. He won't get here for another three hours. Maman draws the window curtains and I stretch out, grateful for the dim light. For once, heaven is on my side.

~~~~~~~~

It's three in the afternoon. I couldn't swallow a thing at lunch. I told my mother I felt sick to my stomach. I'm in bed, in my pajamas. I mustn't fall asleep. I try to read, to concentrate on the words as hard as I can. The cleaning lady brings me a glass of water. When Maman and I were yelling yesterday, Monique had looked quite uncomfortable. She places a hesitant hand on my forehead, which isn't hot at all—in fact, I feel colder and colder. She asks me how I'm doing and suddenly I'm deeply moved by her concern. I take that warm hand and lay it against my cheek, saying softly, "Don't worry, I've arranged everything, it won't happen again."

Two minutes later, my mother bursts into my room and shakes me roughly.

"What did you tell Monique? What have you done this time?"

It's her "this time" that shuts my mouth tight.

I no longer try to look her in the eyes. I close mine and wait for her to leave.

Today feels as if it will never end. To wake up, I splash a little water on my face. I long dreadfully to sleep. I turn on the radio, loud. In a fake, jolly voice, an announcer is translating the lyrics to a Beatles song. We don't love them for their *words*, you jerk!

I must have drifted off because I'm startled by the touch of Dr. Assan's cold hands on my temples. I open my eyes to his salt-and-pepper eyebrows, his impassive gaze. He applies his stethoscope, listens to my heart, takes my pulse and says, holding my wrists, "You can talk to me, you know. I'm a doctor."

I glance at his watch. Twenty past four. I swallowed everything at eight o'clock, so that should do it.

Then, doing my best, tripping over words I can barely pronounce now, I tell him about the medicine cabinet, the empty boxes thrown away as I walked to school, the big glasses of water.

He looks at his watch too, stands up abruptly, packs his things. He has the inscrutable face of someone who must swiftly make a difficult decision. Before leaving the room, he looks at me sadly, and I measure the weight I have just placed on his shoulders.

I'd like to tell him I'm so sorry to saddle him with this, when he's had nothing to do with it. But my energy's all gone. My tongue is even more sluggish than my brain. My jaws feel encased in plaster; my mouth won't open anymore. By the time I've sized up my situation, the doctor has left.

So I give up. I slide into a night without dreams. My body is now just a lump of cotton wool. I feel myself falling into a void that sucks me in without a sound.

There, I've done it. Everything will return to its proper place.

Them here. Me over there.

I hear the alarm clock on the night table.

I tell myself that it's ticking too loudly, louder than my heart that has almost stopped beating.

The second hand of the alarm clock.

That's the last thing I remember.

Part One

Opaque black stockings, with a seam that ran from the heel all the way up the back of the leg. I noticed them right away when my mother came into my room. I was quite feverish, with a bad case of the flu. I'd been flat on my back in bed for five days. I watched her legs, fascinated. My mother always dressed discreetly, with midcalf-length skirts and gray tights. Those stockings gave her an unfamiliar and sophisticated allure.

Instead of coming to sit on the edge of my bed, she paced back and forth, and the room swayed to the rhythm of her dark skirt.

Only then did I notice, in the buttonhole of her navy blue blouse, a tiny bit of black crepe she was fiddling with nervously.

"Do you know what this means?" she asked.

She was using the voice from her bad days: a touch dry, short of breath, the voice for when she's trying to get a grip on herself, on her nerves, her fatigue.

That morning, it was her grief she was trying to keep under control.

I felt my heart shrink in my chest and my throat tighten in anguish.

She was intensely agitated.

I pulled the covers up to my chin before answering, as briefly as possible: "Does it mean someone has just died?"

She became still, finally, but would not meet my eyes.

"Yes, someone in the family."

I sensed that she was waiting for me to guess, to understand, but my mind was muddled by fear.

We had some old aunts in Israel . . . it was probably one of them . . . No, that wouldn't put her in this state . . . Ah, I had it: it must be the old lady who took care of her when she was twenty, and whom she loved like a grandm—

"It's your grandfather."

She paused, took a deep breath and, released from the burden of her news, blurted everything out.

"He came home from a trip on Monday, you know that. But he didn't feel well and he died that night. We buried him yesterday afternoon, you were asleep, you didn't ask me where I was. It's very young to die, sixty-three; you know how I adored him, so think of him, he loved you very much. The doctor's coming soon; you'd best take your temperature. You seem better this morning, so should I bring you breakfast or do you want to get up?"

I took the rectal thermometer, slipped it under the sheet, and turned toward the wall.

"I'll leave you now; there are so many things to sort out and problems to deal with, you can imagine. I'll pop in later."

The door closed quietly.

Even lying down, I could feel my legs trembling. The noise from the street was muffled now, like the notes of a piano when the strings are covered with a velvet rug to avoid disturbing the neighbors. My heart, pounding so wildly a minute ago, had stopped short and seemed to beat only in fits and starts.

I sat up suddenly. Perhaps that position would help my brain cope with the unspeakable. But nothing did.

My mind was reeling, stymied by a single thought, like a worn needle stuck in a record groove . . .

Four whole days ago.

Ninety-six hours of oblivion, during which I read, ate, and slept as usual when the best part of my life had vanished forever.

I don't know what hurt more: the grief, or not even knowing he'd died. Delayed-action mourning is more crushing. It has lost all cadence, all rhythm, and is experienced outside the cycle of days and nights, of people who cry and people who console.

Everything had been said, wailed, wept without me.

My sorrow was outside of time, and thus infinite.

The black stockings had dealt a death blow to my childhood.

The following Monday, back in school, I found the news had preceded me. I was welcomed with suspect kindness and consideration. I had few friends; I'd gotten used to that. As the smallest as well as the youngest girl, I understood why no one wanted to be seen with the class "baby." Ever since I was eight, I'd been a year ahead of my age group in school, but that meant my life felt as if it were a year behind those of my classmates and their jokes, secrets, pre-occupations. Their sudden solicitude, a mixture of pity and condescension, was exasperating.

"So, are you feeling better? Poor thing, you must be sad! Were you very fond of your grandpa?"

Fists clenched in the pockets of my gray school smock, I made an effort not to be disagreeable, clenching my teeth to keep from saying something sarcastic.

All the girls saw my silence as proof of my sorrow.

"Look, you see, she's really sad!" they murmured, with sidelong glances at me between bites of their afternoon snacks.

I had no use for their brand-new interest in me. It had come too late. Between them and me, between their indifference and my shyness, their united front and my fear of never winning them over, a gulf had opened like a wound that hurts only when touched.

What separated us this time was a question of vocabulary, for which there was no answer.

What words could reveal that the problem was not the death of a grandfather, but a world shaken on its axis, a sky scraped raw, a pure note turned strident, abandonment beyond all measure?

How to explain that it hurt so much?

And whose business was it anyway?

He gave me terrible nicknames, which made me angry, and my anger made him laugh. His laughter was big, strong, enveloping, like his hands when they helped me untie the knots of the packages that were always waiting for me when I visited him.

In his bedroom was a low chest with five drawers, and the bottom one was reserved for me. I could arrive unexpectedly, yet find a surprise hidden there every time. A gift, a handkerchief, a lollipop, it could be anything.

That was a promise he'd made me and he never once broke it. That permanently restocked drawer represented the infallible proof of his love for me.

He did not treat me like a granddaughter, like a little girl. He considered me a person with whom to share and exchange things to read, points of view, essential discoveries.

For example, when I was six, and the two of us were having lunch in his kitchen, he placed before me a white plate bearing a regal *chèvre cendré*. He knew that I hated cheese in general and this kind in particular, because to me goat cheese tasted like soap. He was immensely fond of *chèvre cendré*, however, so it was impossible that his granddaughter should not share this predilection. He uncorked a bottle of Bordeaux, placed a bit of *chèvre* on a small piece of warm toast lightly spread with salted butter, and explained to me precisely how the flavor of the cheese would be accentuated by the wine's acidity. His blue-footed wineglass clinked mine to celebrate my first tasting as a connoisseur, in the certainty that from then on, just as we shared a straight nose, drooping eyelids, and the inveterate habit of constantly humming, his favorite cheese would also be mine.

He was facetious, imperious. He understood everything and I could tell him frightening secrets he would never have thought to make fun of. He was not judgmental, never reproving, and aside from lapses in good manners, about which he was intransigent, he was quick to forgive. Mockery was his usual tack, repartee his besetting sin, generosity his Achilles' heel. His humor made the world cozier, his tenderness cushioned my days. Nothing could ever happen to me as long as he was there, and I had never envisaged a life without him as its center.

He called me his "sunshine," but it was mine he took away with him.

I was what is called a good child. I continued to be one.

No one noticed that I was turning inward, withdrawing inside myself.

I was calm. I became silent.

I had been lonely. Now I was alone.

In the weeks that followed the news of his death, no one mentioned my grandfather. At least not in front of me.

Often, when I was in the kitchen to set the table or else reading off by myself, I would hear my mother and sister, behind the closed double doors of the living room, recalling old memories and sometimes breaking down, stifling their sobs. And I would have given anything to laugh and cry with them. But I would have swallowed my tongue rather than say that.

It would never have occurred to me to cross the hall, open the double doors, and tell them the stories that were feeding my grief.

"You don't sit down at a table where you haven't been invited," my grandfather would have said with a nod of approval.

In my presence, my family bore up under their loss. My sister distracted my father with her algebra problems, while my mother alternated between cooking and housework with robotic efficiency to keep her sorrow at bay. Everyone had the same mission: to spare "the little one" the painful burdens of the grown-ups.

They meant well, which is the excuse offered whenever a good intention goes awry.

The effect, on me, was radical.

Since I wasn't worthy of weeping with them, they'd get nothing from me. Neither laughter nor tears. Not one secret shared. I would barely be there.

I became transparent. Present, but elsewhere. Polite but reserved. Pleasantly indifferent. I would reveal no more of myself.

I kept my distance, the way a prisoner digs a hole at the far end of the cell, scratching away a few millimeters every day: too little to be noticed but enough to keep spirits up.

I didn't want to arouse any suspicions.

So I became nice.

Too nice.

In repeated doses, niceness can be suspect, close to simplemindedness. Since nothing ever disturbed my docility, I wound up giving the impression of being rather vacant.

Since the three members of my family were essentially somewhere else, in a bubble separate from mine, I thought of them as "the people across the way," and little by little, they allowed themselves to be fooled by what I let them see. By continually retreating within myself, I had bleached out all my colors. Wanting to be invisible, I was henceforth insipid.

The misapprehension was under way.

A few months later, Uncle Émile came to visit us. He was my grandfather's elder brother. They resembled each other physically, but the one was like a distorting mirror of the other, his negative copy, Cain to his Abel, his shadow face, his dark angel. Émile's burliness was vaguely threatening, and his geniality a façade to mask his cunning. Even his brand of humor veered into malice. Everything supple, ample, and generous in the younger man became brittle and stiff in his brother. And his booming laughter could be chilling.

But until that March morning when, freezing in our Sunday best, we waited in pounding rain for the

Brussels–Paris train to enter the station, I had never realized how much I disliked him. For one simple reason: he'd had no place in my life, nor I in his. I suppose that during my childhood we'd sniffed around each other, backed off, and without acrimony left it at that, perfectly synchronized in our mutual indifference.

Unconsciously, I had registered everything, stashing it away in some drowsy compartment of my brain that came suddenly to life and disgorged its flood of bad impressions the moment those gleaming black patent-leather oxfords stepped down off the train, bearing an imposing form tightly cinched into a fawn-colored cashmere coat.

A porter materialized immediately to take charge of the leather-strapped beige canvas luggage to which Émile pointed with his kid-gloved fingertips before wrapping his arms around the damp shoulders of my mother's peacoat in a theatrical embrace.

"My poor dear, I'm here now, ready to devote all my time to you."

But he never noticed the distress in mother's little face, busy as he was inspecting all the passing women under forty, automatically taking inventory of their charms and flaws with the sharp eye of a professional who, even in his leisure moments, could not stop sizing up the situation: pretty legs . . . flirtatious . . . unhappy marriage . . . nose job. More of a meat inspector than a sensualist, my uncle stared at those women with cold precision, and I blushed for them. Clutching his arm, my mother saw nothing, shaken by that face so like her father's, happy to be the main object of his visit, even if it had taken tragic circumstances for him to finally grant her his exclusive attention.

In French novels there are exotic and distant uncles from America possessing fortunes obscurely acquired and regularly exaggerated. In our family, the uncle came from Belgium and, thanks to him, we endowed that flat country with every marvel. Émile was the only one of us who had succeeded. He had built his fortune out of the stuff of legends: jewels.

He shone out over our family like an overlarge diamond, tacky and mysterious.

Of his past, I knew only that the war had surprised him far from his native Austria and that Belgium was where he'd managed to hide. Was he forced to change his name during the war, or had that come later? Had he done it out of gratitude toward the country that had sheltered him, or to facilitate his integration there? In any case, he no longer shared anything more with my grandfather than a capital letter, having traded in the rest of the family name for a surname that sounded more Flemish than Walloon and not Viennese at all.

Anvers was where he had made his fortune and his reputation.

Various anecdotes all exalted this exemplary success, unique in the annals of our family. For Central European Jews who had not had time to emigrate far from the swastikas, it was already a miracle to have escaped death.

Émile was the only one who hadn't settled for mere survival.

People claimed he was immensely wealthy. Lowering their voices, they would say that when the biggest diamond merchants in the world got together for an informal precious stones market, they examined the jewels one dealer at a time following a hierarchy reflecting their status in the profession. My uncle was the ninth to select his stones, and to be ninth, opined the adults with the knowing air of novices hoping to pass for experts, was incredible. Tongues wagged furiously over the famous women who were his clients and the liaisons he'd supposedly enjoyed with some of them. He had married for love a woman he kept in fearful submission, alternating between showering her with princely gifts and pitching fits of jealousy, when he wasn't having Homeric tantrums over the sums she spent on haute couture.

The ninth-biggest diamond merchant in the world was surely among the top three skinflints of the century. His stinginess was as legendary as his financial acumen.

He could have taken one of the finest suites at the Ritz by the year in Paris, a city he loved to visit. He preferred to stay in a place on the corner of our street and take his meals with us.

"It's because he has a sense of family," explained my mother, who spent the week before his arrival scrubbing our tiny apartment from stem to stern. There is spring cleaning, and there's getting ready for winter, but in our home, there was also the "Belgian clean sweep," when a visit from Émile prompted us to bring out our best clothes and china so as not to suffocate under the weight of our inferiority. And I hated him from the bottom of my heart for humiliating my mother that way.

~~~~~~~~~

This time, my uncle came neither for business nor to renew his wardrobe but solely for his niece, as he was now her closest relative.

He stayed four days and had long conferences with my parents from which my mother emerged with reddened eyes, her shoulders bowed with the weight of her gratitude.

He took her along when he went shopping, forced her to accompany him to the theater. And on the last day grandly announced that he was taking us all to lunch.

His favorite brasserie wasn't much to look at, but it served, he insisted authoritatively, the best leg of lamb in Europe. No need to consult the menu: lamb all around. My sister was allowed to wet her lips with bloodred nectar served in tulip glasses; when I was tactless enough to ask for some sparkling mineral water, he ordered a carafe of plain water for *la petite*. My request was the only time I spoke during the meal, my mother's angry look having clearly informed me that I was decidedly lacking in manners.

Bent over my plate, avoiding their eyes, I stewed in my bitterness. My grandfather, now, *he* wouldn't have said a thing. Besides, he hated restaurants, found them noisy. He claimed that one couldn't put all the senses into play at the same time and that to savor a dish required silence, even contemplation.

My uncle paid such considerations no mind. He was a talker at the table, trumpeting his observations with a loud familiarity, summoning the waiters, using the informal *tu* with the maître d', slipping into the kitchen after the cheese course to tip all the apprentices. But he left my mother to pay for the taxi home.

He came up to our apartment to have a digestive liqueur and we all settled into the living room to kill some time before accompanying him back to the station for the evening train. Perched on a footstool with a book on my lap, I pretended to read but did not miss one bit of those adult conversations, which for once were taking place in my presence.

My uncle talked about a childhood memory, an argument with his brother about a brand-new bike he'd damaged on purpose out of jealousy, since the bike was a reward for the younger boy's excellent grades, which were better than his brother's. I could sense the antagonism lurking in that story, the furious competition that all the older brother's fortune had not managed to erase. And I listened in vain to that nasal voice for the right note of true family affection.

Deep in my hostile thoughts, I felt myself flush when I heard him say abruptly, "Now, leave me alone with *la petite*."

Keeping my head down, I didn't dare look up from *The Black Stallion*. He took the book gently from my hands and sat down in front of me.

"You're terribly sad, aren't you?"

His voice was soft, no longer wheezy at all. He placed his hands on mine.

I gritted my teeth and prayed to the gods not to let me cry in front of him.

"I know how much you adored my brother, and he often talked about you. So I also came here to tell you this: you can count on me. I will never replace him for you, but I will do my best to be worthy of him. I will visit more often, we'll do things together. You'll tell me which books you like and we'll go pick out others you don't know. In the meantime, we'll write to each other."

He took me in his arms. I smelled the woody scent of his eau de cologne, and that autumnal perfume made me want to be won over. Yes, I asked nothing better than to believe him, to love him. I put my arms around his neck and hugged him as hard as I could, touched by his unexpected kindness, like a caress from heaven. After all, the same blood in his veins had run in my grandfather's. He couldn't possibly hurt me.

The next day, carried away, emboldened, I decided to send him a card to thank him for talking with me. I often wrote to my grandfather. He used to tell me that he loved hearing from me, and he had carefully saved the note in which, instead of signing "Your granddaughter who adores you," I had written "Your adored granddaughter." He had phoned me as soon as he'd received it: "That's true, I do adore you, so you can write that!"

I took great care with my handwriting when I wrote to Émile to avoid even a single mistake, so that he would be proud of me, his brother's favorite, and would want to write me back.

I hoped for a letter, a phone call.

I waited. Expectantly. Particularly around special occasions, holidays, vacations, trips.

Six months later, he never even thought to wish me a happy ninth birthday.

It was around that time that I began to write. I filled whole notebooks with the blue ink of the South Seas. All this writing wasn't the sign of a precocious talent, but an overflow of unspoken words that were stifling me.

Since I was no longer speaking to anyone, I had invented a confidante with whom I conversed on familiar terms, a sweet creature I baptized Laure. I loved that name for its aura of infinite gentleness. Laure. *Laure* . . . I whispered it like a soothing prayer.

Laure was who I would have liked to be. A slender elf, gentle and mischievous, a model for a desperately ordinary little girl.

Ever since my first year of school, I had faced this fact: I would never be pretty. I had none of those classic features described in novels. Neither the delicate nose, nor the prominent cheekbones, the high forehead, the rosebud mouth, the almond eyes, the silken tresses. My mostly straight nose had a bump that ruined its profile. My high-enough forehead only accentuated a wandering eye made more obvious by round glasses. My ears stuck out, my chin was too pointy, my teeth were uneven. I looked like what I was: a run-of-the-mill child.

Inside me, though, there was Laure. And Laure had a special grace, the grace that makes people look at you instead of just seeing you, and listen to you instead of merely hearing you. She had strength, enough to carry the weight of my dreams. And they were vast.

I wanted everything. To write. Sing. Invent. Compose. I had no desire for power, only a thirst to be someone—as well as the terror of not succeeding in that, plus the certainty that I would not survive such a failure. I was exalted by what I felt ready to accomplish but ashamed for even daring to imagine that one day, the world might come knocking at my door and sweep me up in its whirl.

A life that's worthwhile ... How does one deserve that?

All my notebooks to Laure were full of those incantations. For lack of a destiny, I had a heroine of invincible beauty with legitimate ambitions. She gave me the armor in which I felt encouraged to go off to every battle. With her, I was fearless.

In the evening, the family apartment was divided in two, each side retrenched in its territory. My parents and sister gathered around the living room television. Behind my closed door, a radio was my spyglass pointed at the future, that inaccessible world of adulthood my transistor made palpable, concrete.

The radio was my lifeline, the instrument of my escape, my tutor, and I was its attentive pupil. A radio brings within reach of the imagination a world in black and white where you are free to invent colors, contours, reliefs, like a kaleidoscope turned endlessly before your eyes by an invisible hand. Since the radio speaks to no one in particular, it persuades you that it addresses you alone. It couldn't care less that you're too young, too ugly, and nothing special. It confides in you. It trusts you. It tells you everything it knows, right away.

I realized this one evening in November when I flung open the living room door and announced that President Kennedy had just been assassinated. My parents froze; my sister raised a suspicious eyebrow.

"You're sure you've got that right?"

I returned to my lair without deigning to reply, intoxicated at having been, for the first time, the one in the know, an adult among my peers. Since information was power, Laure would now have a profession: journalism.

She says her first memory is when I was brought home: she was three, and I was five days old. She had a pretty room with cream wallpaper and stuffed animals massed at the foot of her crib. It was nap time.

Because of a mix-up, my cradle had not yet been delivered. My mother set me down in the crib.

My sister says she remembers her rage.

A week later, she began nursery school, leaving behind this newborn who was taking over her bed, her mother, the whole place.

She says she remembers her misery.

She reigned over my childhood like a queen bee. She was the sun I admired from the shadows. She had presence, talent, and was always first in the class. Admired by everyone, she saw herself in the mirror of their love. I studied her secretly, the way one observes an unknown species, with curiosity but not jealousy, because you cannot want to be like something you don't understand. To me she was the most unfathomable of mysteries. I could not figure out how her brain worked, or her soul. I found her beautiful. She had about her a strength that was too precise, too violent for our cramped apartment, our little lives, as if the stork had somehow delivered her to the wrong address. The deference shown to my sister by grown-ups only enhanced this vision of her as a treasure made ours through some miracle.

She was precocious, as if she'd been born having already attained the age of reason. Beneath her gleaming helmet of black hair, her brain gloried in her overwhelming intellect. When she spoke, adults made much of her opinions. By the time I'd put a few thoughts in order, I'd already lost the chance to get a word in edgewise.

I grew used to keeping quiet and listening to her. Used to contemplating the radiance of her striking loveliness. A strong profile, aquiline nose, firm chin, and a crisp bob hairstyle reinforced her self-confidence. She knew. She ruled the world. She was the Alice of a land where she was the unique and priceless wonder. My sister the prodigy.

She was the idol of my childhood. More than my mother or father, she was the one I would have liked to dazzle and astonish. Or simply surprise. I was like a puppy wanting to be petted but unable to decide whether to sit up and beg or pee all over the place.

I pestered her with questions. I followed her everywhere. The most clinging of little sisters. Her humblest subject.

Occasionally, I rebelled. But she was too powerful. She always found just the right word, the one that cuts home, wounds, knocks the wind out of you, leaving you disarmed and vanquished. She didn't need me. I needed her too much.

> *Once upon a time there was a queen*
> *Adored by a dwarf girl, pining unseen,*
> *For how could a humble creature so small*
> *Captivate the loveliest queen of them all?*
> *Yet to a knight who appeared one day,*
> *The queen gave her royal heart away.*

"Sir knight, on whom our queen doth dote,
Would you kindly tell her, so she may note,
That the dwarf girl, of most modest station,
Adores her with blindest admiration?
Tell her, I beg you, for I cannot
Make myself heard from my lowly spot."

The queen and the dwarf girl. That's how I saw us. How to win the love of the queen when you're only the dwarf? I wore out my nerves over this. I worried so much I forgot to grow.

The queen knew how to be cruel. She often withheld the keys to words whose meaning she did not wish to explain to me. When I was eleven and we were off on a skiing vacation, I managed to snag a stool at the end of a table where she was having lunch with some kids her own age, after our mother had pleaded my case with her along the well-known lines of, "She's your sister, after all!"

The older kids were talking about astrology. My neighbor, a freckle-faced boy, was kind enough to ask me what my sign was. And when I murmured, blushing to be suddenly the center of attention, "I'm a Virgin," the queen's laughter drowned out everyone else's, as I sank into disaster without a word from her. Humiliated by their hilarity, unable to understand what was so funny, I kept repeating, louder and louder, until I was screaming in that ski resort restaurant gone abruptly silent, "I'm a Virgin!"

The queen let me make a fool of myself without lifting a finger to rescue me. That evening, she lost the unconditional devotion of her most faithful subject.

Since she was gifted at everything and I at not much, she became my tutor (for a slight increase in her allowance). She was not a good teacher. My inability to quickly grasp what she was hurriedly explaining to me exasperated her, and her impatience paralyzed my brain, for my shame at not understanding was so overwhelming that it swept all thoughts from my head: I was petrified. Each lesson left me even more foolish, more dwarfed, before the queen who would sail from the room with her chin in the air, abandoning me to my fate the way a wild animal discards its prey after ripping apart the carcass. Once again she had won, in addition to some extra pocket money, the assurance that she had no rival for her crown.

"Mirror, mirror, on the wall, am I still the best of all?"

"Yes," admitted the girl left holding the mirror for her, crumpled in defeat.

From the sixth grade on, I found myself in the same lycée as my sister. I was not a good student. I did the bare minimum, just enough to avoid repeating a year, not enough to win the slightest honor. And honors, that's precisely what my sister collected, enough that her name had become a guarantee of quality that I was rapidly ruining. So the disappointed teachers who'd found me in their classes took their revenge on my report card.

"Not as good as her sister," was the blunt assessment of a French teacher who'd never actually had her in his class.

"Makes us miss her elder sibling," sniffed the math teacher.

"She'll have problems!" prophesied the history-geography teacher.

I had no talent for anything, except music.

"But those grades aren't enough to bring her average up," was the concluding comment from the principal.

On report card days, I was careful to miss the bus, dodging the half-inquisitive, half-triumphant "Well?" from the helmet of black hair, and I walked home, choosing the longest route, waiting for lights to turn green, even helping the blind people from a nearby institute negotiate the crosswalks.

On those days, I begged my grandfather's pardon, for just the thought of him made me blush with shame. I promised heaven I'd do better. The next day, though, after the first hour of class, all my good resolutions went out the window, and my concentration with them. I was bored, I daydreamed, I lost track of the lesson and never managed to pick it up again. As soon as I entered a classroom, my mind wandered off to play hooky.

Thanks to all my flights of fancy and scribbled notebooks to Laure, I was skilled at writing fairly effortless essays on those prescribed topics that are the lot of lycée students from the sixth grade on. But this rare scholastic pleasure vanished on the day when, to evoke the "autumn landscape" in an essay, I wrote, "The oaks that, bending in the winds, lean their heads together to whisper secrets in one another's ears."

Rather satisfied with my twenty lines, I waited impatiently for the results of my efforts, hoping for a grade high enough to raise my class standing. Alas, the distribution of the papers in descending order of merit passed without my name being called. I was about to raise my hand, hoping I'd simply been forgotten, when the teacher forestalled me with a swift jerk of her chin.

"You will come see me after class."

The rest of which dragged on in slow motion, punctuated by the heartbeats I heard pounding in my temples.

I waited until all my classmates had gone before approaching the teacher's desk. She avoided my eyes while carefully stowing her papers away in her fake green crocodile briefcase.

The croc snapped shut with a dry click as she asked me brusquely, "So, you're fond of Victor Hugo?"

She finally looked up and leaned in close to my pale face.

"I hate cheaters. Victor Hugo described the 'whispering trees' much better than you did. So do me a favor and leave his idea to him."

She stood up with a stamp of her platform shoes.

"I will not report you. I gave you a zero. Next time do your own thinking, instead of trying to impress your teachers."

With that, she slipped on her beige raincoat with a plaid lining and left me alone, crushed.

I'd never read a single line of Victor Hugo.

But bad students are not given the benefit of the doubt.

I was too much of a dunce in her eyes to have come up on my own with an idea so banal that a great poet had already immortalized it, unbeknownst to me.

In my eyes, a gift for literature—and music as well—was the most noble talent anyone could possess. I believed I had a feeling for le mot juste, just as I had a good ear. That morning, I understood that I'd greatly overestimated myself.

I was unworthy, inferior, without distinction. True, I played Chopin from memory and blackened entire notebooks with Laure's adventures, but what I thought were my good ideas was only the pallid recycling of the works of great authors.

Until that moment, I'd thought I was a poor pupil because I didn't pay enough attention. For the first time, I had to accept the general opinion: it wasn't my ability to concentrate that was limited but my comprehension itself.

Luckily, Grandfather was no longer there to witness the end of my ambitions, the collapse of my self-respect, the nightmarish end of my literary dreams.

Grandfather had been mistaken.

To appease my fury, I spent the whole of the following recreation period composing an "Ode to the Teaching Establishment," which I intended to slide anonymously under the door of the teachers' lounge, but the fear of being expelled sent this short text to swell the pile of handwritten pages known only to Laure.

> *You hate me,*
> *Toads, vipers,*
> *But you will not silence me.*
> *I know that you envy me*
> *The life flowing in my veins.*

La Petite

For I, I intend to live,
And that pains you no end.

It was all mere bravado. Live, me? Dying of boredom in school, then making myself as small as could be, keeping my thoughts to myself at home—that wasn't living. More like wasting away.

The main thing from now on was to avoid being noticed under any circumstances. It was better to live like a mouse does, quietly in its hole. I resolved not to bother anyone anymore, not to disturb the peaceful routine either at school or at home.

I wished to be alone with my dreams left in tatters.

A plagiarist, even an inadvertent one, has no right to a glittering life. Let her be content to nibble on whatever she can find. Songs played on the radio and books lent graciously by the municipal library, two per week, and four during vacations.

I organized my days for my own protection. I fed on the imaginations, the daily lives, the music of others. Thus comforted, I forgot about my sorry little self, my mediocrity in school, my dwarf's motley rags, and Grandfather's chest, now installed in our living room, where the bottom drawer held only a sewing basket.

When it was dark, I would turn out the light, bring my transistor into bed and, entranced by the soul music played every night by an English radio station, I'd fall asleep trying to believe that maybe the next day wouldn't be as grim as the last one had been.

At that age, I often had the same nightmare.

I was at the movies, by myself, sitting in the middle of a row. The theater was full. The film must have been a comedy, because everyone was laughing. Except me.

The crimson seats were all attached to one another. When the spectators leaned back to howl with glee, they made the seats tip toward the black and roiling ocean behind us.

We were all going to drown. I stared in terror at those faces twisted with mirth, at that dark water into which my hair was about to fall, and I thought,

"Why do I have to die with them when I didn't get to laugh?"

And I don't know whether I was sadder at dying for no good reason or for not having learned how to laugh with all the others.

To be or not to be like everyone else.

Did I have to choose one side or the other to stop being *la petite* and finally grow up?

At eleven, I began looking at the boys who came to get the girls when school let out.

Me, I knew men, the real ones: those in my favorite novels, like *Rebecca* or *Jalna*, the first book in a long sentimental saga about the Whiteoak family of Canada. Such men were fierce and fiery creatures who lowered their guard only to sweep lovesick women into their embrace, women who clung to them like drowning souls saved at last from their virginity or conjugal boredom.

Even with my eyes closed I could have drawn their smoldering good looks and, above all, their hands. I dreamed of those hands that stroke and strike, chastise and caress. Hands that mold destinies, hands that trace and disrupt the course of lives, hands that find their place on this earth. In my opinion, one recognized a man by his handshake: bold, gruff, and warm, a hand open like a door onto an unknown world.

The pimple-faced boys who invaded the café-bar across from the lycée had sweaty palms, nails bitten to the quick, chin hair, and minds as stiff and inflexible as their navy blue coats.

I considered them with contempt. Those scrawny jerks whose voices were still shuttling between treble and bass were not the stuff of my dreams, and I didn't understand how they could inspire the constant stream of notes the girls in my class exchanged with knowing glances.

I was automatically excluded from this ferment. Most of those girls had curves under their tight Shetland sweaters, tampons in their purses, liner on their eyelids, and very precise notions regarding male anatomy.

I'd stopped believing in the stork when I abandoned Santa Claus, but I still didn't understand the meaning of the magic formula in books that made men cry out and women sigh, that paroxysm about which whole pages were written without ever saying exactly what it was, the obstacle course that—depending on the author—took two hours or three minutes, left women bitter or fulfilled, but very often pregnant, turned the heads of the most virtuous among them, and could drive the most levelheaded to the brink of madness: "making love." What did that mean, concretely, technically? Whom could I ask?

Parents lowered their voices when speaking of such things, and the advice to the lovelorn in women's magazines was no more explicit. Where could I turn? None of the reputedly racy novels satisfied my curiosity. As for the Shetland set, their conversations were devoted exclusively to one question that governed a definitive hierarchy among them: who had already tongue-kissed? Those who had could pride themselves on "dating" a boy.

One day in January when I'd taken the next day's homework assignments to a sick classmate, her apartment door was opened by a boy with gray eyes, curly brown hair, and that lucky gap between his upper front teeth. The way he took the ring binder from my hands gave me a strange twinge in my stomach.

Richard was an eighth grader and lived two blocks from the lycée; we would meet when school let out so he could get that day's homework for his sister who, thank God, had scarlet fever and so would be absent for two weeks.

It wasn't much, but it was enough to start tongues wagging all the way to the ears of the queen, who summoned me to her room for an interrogation. Yes, I heard myself lying shamelessly, yes, of course, I was going out with him! The queen smiled haughtily.

That evening, in the kitchen, my mother observed—with fake offhandedness, studying the made-in-England toaster that never toasted, only burned the bread: "Your sister told me. You're getting an early start, I must say!"

The heating element inside the toaster never glowed as red as my cheeks did. I could have whipped myself for shame. I didn't even dare write to Laure about it. How could I have done that? How do you confess that you never committed the fault you bragged you were guilty of?

The cheater was a liar.

To rub it in, I stood in front of the bathroom mirror. A gray mouse in brown glasses. Nothing to sustain Richard's attention.

My mother's remark had hit home like a door slamming shut.

The world of boys would have to do without me.

For our summer vacation, we joined Uncle Émile in Knokke-le-Zoute.

That seaside resort is to Brussels what Deauville is to Paris: the beach closest to the capital and therefore the most snobbish and expensive one. Instead of a boardwalk and picturesque Norman half-timbering, Knokke could boast a white stucco casino where the French pop singer Adamo appeared regularly and a red stone dike running along the beach all the way to Holland, which made a marvelous bike path for children my age. Of course, Knokke-le-Zoute did not sound like an overly attractive destination to my classmates, who

found the name ridiculous, at least until Jacques
Brel ennobled it at last in his "Chanson de Jacky"
in 1966.

Even if one day, at Knokke-le-Zoute,
I wind up doing my best to look cute
Singing to ladies who've seen better days . . .

In Knokke, the North Sea wind blew in gusts that
could knock you off your feet. The town smelled like
iodine, waffles, and the mayonnaise used to stuff
tomatoes, which were a local delicacy. Instead of
croissants, for breakfast there were little round rolls,
still warm when split open to be spread with salted
butter, and on mornings when I felt brave enough to
pedal off after eight o'clock to the main fish store, we
had freshly shelled shrimp as well.

My preferred vehicle was a bicycle. Plenty of merchants on the dike had surreys, bikes for more than
one person, which they rented by the hour and at a
stiff price. These were like pedal boats for roads, and
the locals had slyly nicknamed them ThighCabs. To
the children's delight, these vehicles designed for
large families were equipped with thunderous horns,

and each store had its own identifying color: apple green, bloodred, or canary yellow.

Time seemed to stretch out with long strolls on the sandy dunes, games of miniature golf, visits to the Zwin nature reserve, and the ritual of tea chez Uncle Émile, who owned a large apartment looking out over the sea.

At the stroke of four, after the parental nap, we would gather in the lobby of our hotel, a spic-and-span but dreary boardinghouse. The square dining room fronted on the street, and the bay windows—without curtains, as is often the case in Belgium—reflected only the pale gray wall of the post office across the way. The dining room offered a buffet at noon and menu seating in the evening, with a bowl of soup as a starter, so the room always smelled of bouillon. A large television sat in a musty parlor with closed blinds. The phone booth was next to the reception desk, where a blond young man with a very pale face, an impassive expression, and lips compressed with concentration eavesdropped with enormous pleasure on the conversations of the clientele.

Since my father preferred to walk rather than bicycle, we went to Uncle Émile's on foot, which took half an hour, after which I felt authorized to take two helpings of *kramik*, a kind of raisin brioche my aunt served piping hot from the oven. The tea service was of black-and-white china, and I never dared pour myself a second cup for fear of spilling even a drop on the cream carpet. Émile was rarely present, and in his absence my aunt monopolized the conversation, speaking very fast as if she dreaded his imminent return.

As for me, I'd long ago given up expecting anything from him.

One year after his visit to Paris, he had left me in charge, in that Brussels apartment, of his twenty-month-old granddaughter, who had awakened an hour after his departure. She was hungry and needed to be changed, but I'd been given neither fresh diapers nor instructions, so I picked her up and to distract her, carried her around the apartment, humming a song. She calmed down, but when she heard a key in the lock, she began to wail. My uncle dashed from the entrance hall, still wearing his hat, kid gloves, and loden coat, and snatched the child from my arms, shouting that I was incompetent and that he would never, ever forgive me for having brought tears to the cheeks of his greatest treasure.

Ever since that episode, we'd never spoken to each other beyond the usual formal greetings.

After helping clear away the tea things, I was often bored and went down a long hall to leaf through the paperback books on the shelves in the master bedroom, where my aunt allowed me to borrow things to read.

It is thus to her that I owe some unforgettable discoveries, including a collection of novellas by Fitzgerald that thrilled me so much my aunt allowed me to keep the dog-eared volume, imbued with the scent of Calèche, by Hermès. I was very fond of my aunt. I admired her for putting up with the daily onslaught of harsh remarks my uncle flung at her. She took no offense, and was extra kind to me, as if she wished to make up for her husband's aggressiveness.

One day when I was alone for a moment in their bathroom, I was washing my hands and looking in the mirror when I noticed that the little chignon I had gone to such trouble to create for that visit, and which definitely looked rather nice on me, was now marred by a single lock of hair that had foolishly decided to stick straight up on the top of my head. A sewing kit was sitting on the edge of the sink. I took out a little pair of round-tip scissors, cut off the irritating hair, and went back to my reading.

An hour later my aunt, who was maniacally neat, noticed a dark spot in her immaculate wastebasket: a lock of brown hair. She went immediately on red alert.

Who had come up with the stupid idea of cutting off a lock of her own hair? The irrationality of the gesture exasperated my aunt's sense of logic. *Who* had been as thoughtless, impulsive, and immature as to do that?

All the evidence pointed to me. My sister and I had dark hair, and *her* impeccable pageboy would never fall prey to an angry pair of scissors. The contempt I saw in my aunt's eyes, however, condemned me to silence. I had resigned myself to being ignored by Émile, but I could not bear to lose my aunt's esteem. She was the only one to look kindly at me, without the slightest reservations, and even if the harm had already been done, I wanted to delay the moment of reckoning.

I denied everything.

The more my aunt and mother insisted, the deeper I went into lies, going so far as to feel offended that anyone should doubt my word.

Once more, shame wrung my heart.

Shame for having lied, for lacking courage.

What point was there in living when one was so afraid to be oneself?

And I was afraid of everything. Of boys' kisses, my aunt's disapproval, my sister's laughter, the look in my mother's eyes.

It was only with my grandfather that I'd never feared a thing.

That evening, when I turned out the light, I thought for the first time how good it would be to join him.

Ours was a very small family. Nazism had cut down almost all the branches of our genealogical tree. Besides Uncle Émile, there were only my father's brothers, living in Israel, whom we never saw and whose presence was ritually honored through the sky-blue airmail letters my father exchanged with them every week. He would slit each one open with a paper knife, delicately, taking care as he unfolded it not to tear the precious sheet of tissue-thin paper that served as a prestamped envelope with only limited space for text, like a recto without a verso, while offering the possibility of adding marginal notes on the side flaps, so that the message could be read from top to bottom, then turned in every direction.

The Hebrew characters in the airmail letters reinforced for me the solemn aspect of these exotic missives my father eagerly awaited every Thursday morning, and to which he replied that very evening, bent awkwardly over the corner of a chest of drawers even though he would have been more comfortable sitting at the dining room table. The chest was where he liked to write, however, beneath the harsh light of a too-powerful bulb that allowed him to decipher the small print in *Le Monde* without putting on his glasses.

My father was the head of the family, in the moral sense of the term. An upright man of scrupulous honesty. He left for work at seven thirty, came home at around seven in the evening, gray with fatigue, and it would never have occurred to me to discuss my moods and feelings with him.

I've always felt that my character was close to his, and I sensed, without ever having experienced it, his weariness, a lassitude so burdensome that making conversation was simply beyond his powers.

The weight of Jewish tradition had doubtless accustomed him to the rule of women in the home; be that as it may, outside of important decisions concerning the larger questions of his children's education or an extraordinary household expense, he left our daily lives in my mother's hands, and she acquitted herself with exhausting efficiency. Father made sure that we respected his own values but never interfered in our lives unless my mother considered a problem serious enough to warrant his attention.

Which occurred in particular three times a year, with the arrival of my report cards.

My father had tried everything: scoldings, promises of rewards, anger, contempt, indifference. It would never have crossed his mind to ask me if there was anything wrong. To my parents, psychology was not a school of thought but a well-known medical practice, although a questionable one in the opinion of my mother, who reserved the right to pass judgment on Sigmund Freud, her Viennese compatriot.

In any case, how could I have told my father that I felt estranged from everyone, even him? My lair had become—almost without my realizing it—a cell into which I shut myself more deeply every day and

for which I would have found it impossible to pro-
duce a key.

How could I have described such feelings as loneliness, abandonment, inadequacy—in short, empti-
ness? How could I make a man as staid and steady as
my father understand? His vision of a logical world
of free will in which "where there's a will, there's a
way," was too cut-and-dried to accommodate the
circumvolutions of my inner life.

I was afraid he would judge me.

Only Laure possessed the tolerance I needed. I
could tell her everything.

But she never gave me any answers.

I was going around in circles.

I've always been really bad at math. When I was eleven, in seventh grade, I had a teacher who took a dislike to me. Boredom made me lazy and my presence in her classes was strictly passive. I wanted to become invisible so I wouldn't be hit with her favorite punishment: having to copy out an entire notebook of algebra problems by the next day. The harder I tried to be just a tiny gray mouse, though, the more I sensed that I was getting on her nerves.

After several incidents, a series of bad grades, and a few copied-out notebooks, she decided to summon my mother to discuss my case.

In such situations, my mother backed me up. Whatever my faults, my indolence, my inattention, she defended me in front of teachers, even though she might lecture me after the battle. Against others, she sided with her daughter. So I wasn't worried about her meeting with Mme. Dufour.

My mother returned from her appointment without telling me anything. Not one remark or reproach. No comment.

Toward the end of the afternoon, she informed me that we were going to consult Dr. Assan, our family doctor. I was expecting a routine checkup, a booster shot. Imagine my surprise when the doctor turned to my mother after a routine examination and burst out laughing.

"You can see she hasn't a single problem! It's her teacher I should be examining!"

My mother, reddening and a little embarrassed, was twirling her wedding ring around her finger.

"I'm perfectly aware of that. She's my daughter, after all! But the woman might have noticed something that had escaped us . . ."

Dr. Assan was still chuckling when he walked us to the door.

On the way home, my mother explained that Mme. Dufour thought I was an abnormally slow child, excessively passive, ill adapted, as she'd put it, to the normal school routine. Mme. Dufour believed that I belonged in an institution for special-needs children.

Now that Dr. Assan had reassured her, my mother couldn't speak harshly enough about the negative attitude of a teacher incapable of motivating her students.

What I had learned, though, was that this teacher had managed to make my mother doubt me.

My grandfather had left me two guardian angels: his two best friends. They resembled him. Like him, they each possessed imposing presence, a caustic sense of humor, incontestable charm, and a heart of gold. Like him, they were exiles, unclassifiable, irreducibly themselves, seeking neither assimilation nor recognition. The war had left them with no illusions about human nature. But life—oh, how they loved it! And along with it, women, travel, luxury. And children. The winding course of their lives had deprived them of any offspring.

Their best friend's favorite granddaughter became theirs as well.

They lived abroad and rarely visited.

When they did it was always unexpected, indescribable, unforgettable. Intoxicating.

Together we went to bed late, dined out, tasted new dishes, discovered exotic places: the great couture houses, old bookstores, palaces, gourmet specialty shops. In their wake trailed the echo of their laughter, the warmth of their happiness.

Both of these men, with a smile, a gesture, reawakened in me the gaiety and lightheartedness of bygone days.

It all vanished when they departed, like a mirage. I still had their extravagant gifts, the scent of their cologne, a handkerchief borrowed but never returned, and the feeling of having been, for a few hours, a few days, cherished like a fairy-tale princess.

They were both romantic figures, the heroes of lives richer than many a work of fiction. The first man, whom I always called M. Reuter, was an Austrian, like my grandfather.

Physically, they were much alike. A martial bearing, gray hair, gentle, limpid eyes, undeniable charisma. They had the same rather hefty physique, somewhere between those classic French movie stars Raimu and Jean Gabin. During the 1930s, M. Reuter rented a room from a widow older than he was. This woman, who lived alone with her daughter, became his mistress, and they lived together for several years. She died just when the war broke out.

A Jew, he could no longer remain in Vienna and managed to get out in time.

His landlady's daughter, a sixteen-year-old, was in love with him. She alone knew where he was hiding. For five years, she brought him food and clothing. She saved his life.

After the war, they were married. She was both the woman of his life and the child of his dreams. He was her better in everything: insight, culture, intelligence. Every moment he could spare from his business interests was devoted to her; he forgave her every caprice and was a protective rampart between his wife and the world.

With me, he was attentive and affectionate. An authentic Viennese, a theater lover, and a passionate fan of opera.

My grandfather's other friend, whom everyone called Uncle Dee, had piercing eyes, a receding hairline, and very large ears. He was born in

England. I knew him only as a widower. One day he had taken it into his head to marry an Irish beauty, who'd turned out to suffer from fits of madness. He consulted doctors, turned his home into a clinic. Nothing worked. She wound up confined to an institution. During all those years he had shared an impossible love with his wife's sister, who showed no signs of mental illness. By the time his wife died and he was at last free to marry his sister-in-law, she was ill, and she died without being able to have a child. The London fog was bad for his asthma, so Uncle Dee moved to Jamaica.

His kindness toward me was up to my grandfather's standards. He taught me my first words of English, had me taste my first hamburger. He gave me miraculous gifts out of the blue, like that priceless riding outfit I'd been dreaming of, which he had had delivered to me for my twelfth birthday. He alone could have claimed to be my uncle, that man who was of neither my blood nor my country.

Uncle Dee, like M. Reuter, had made his fortune on his own. Neither man made a big deal out of that. It was simply their revenge against fate, against the shattering of their lives by war. They enjoyed everything like kids, not cynically but with their eyes wide open. Appearing abruptly in our drab lives like magicians, they allowed us to glimpse a refined and cosmopolitan world, where the arts are a pleasure worthy of devotion and life a merry dance in which one must know how to laugh and savor joy. These war-torn survivors were afraid of nothing. At their side, twice a year, I felt indestructible.

~~~~~~

We did not have much money, but we never lacked for anything. My parents knew nothing of frivolity. They did not live for the sake of appearances. They were not spendthrifts. They had chosen to invest everything in their children. My sister and I were to have what they themselves had gone without.

My father would have been satisfied with the quiet daily routine of the middle class. A little house in the Paris region, a dog, a small yard, and a twenty-minute walk to work. That is the life he would have liked to lead and the one my mother made him give up for the sake of his two daughters, since the suburbs offered neither the best schools nor the best society. Since we could not afford the best in everything, we had to decide between our neighborhood and our living space. My mother opted without hesitation for a seven-hundred-and-fifty-square-foot apartment in the upscale shadow of the Eiffel Tower: three rooms for four people as well as the import-export office operating out of our address, for which my mother served as the manager and accountant.

This office became our dining room at mealtimes, and at night, the apple-green convertible armchair where my father liked to make his phone calls unfolded into a bed for me, while my mother's chair at the dinner table became my nightstand. My parents slept in the living room, where the big sofa became a bed as well. Only my sister had a room with a real bed—which she could leave unmade and where she could lie daydreaming—and a door she could close upon her secrets.

Excellence must be cultivated: to flourish it requires effort and a keen sense of priorities. My parents sacrificed the intimacy of a bedroom on the altar of the future. In exchange, my sister made it a point of honor to rise to their expectations. I could hardly complain about that.

Money, clearly, had to be spent cautiously. There was no room for the superfluous in this kind of budget.

I had two passions shared by no one else in my family: music and magazines. I strolled along the stacks of the municipal library, plucking things from any shelf, whatever the category. The only genre I didn't care for was science fiction. I had too many scores to settle with the present to give a hang about the future.

I adored newspapers and all periodicals. Magazines for children, for girls, for dreaming, for playing, for finding the seven things wrong in this passage and solving rebuses, for tapping into the news of the world. A book is eternal, but a newspaper is like the radio, it varies with the times and the fashions, telling the stories of those who have a place in the here and now. I thought newspapers would help me find my place, but my schoolwork wasn't good enough for me to treat myself to them often, especially since I spent all my allowance in the record store.

The radio was the jukebox where I discovered the latest hits, but when you love a song, when you've got it under your skin, you can't be content with simply waiting for it to turn up.

Listening to it—picking it apart, making it completely your own—becomes vitally important.

I was always looking to buy records. I could listen to the same song twenty times in a row. Music was my oxygen.

In a novel by Elsa Triolet where the hero is a pianist, a girl asks him lamely, "Do you love music?"

His reply is both inevitable and implacable. "I make music the way I breathe. Do you love to breathe?"

That's exactly how I felt.

I did my homework to music. I read to music. After dinner, I waited for my parents to go sit down in front of the television. Then I closed the door to the dining room, and all I had to do was turn on my transistor or put on a record to feel at home again. Music defined my space, and I took shelter there.

When my funds melted away too quickly, I busied myself around the apartment doing little chores to earn enough to buy myself two records a month.

I managed to get by, just about.

Until Bernadette turned up in my eighth-grade class.

Bernadette was a touch too chunky for her age. Her straight brown hair was worn parted in the center and held back by two gold barrettes; she often wore kilts and a red checked coat. She lived two blocks away from me.

When one hasn't got a single official pal, a new girl is naturally of interest. Bernadette was low on charm, which lent her a certain luster in my eyes: she had the singular merit of not making me feel more inadequate in her presence. She was taller than I, of course, since I was always the youngest and shortest, but her outdated blouses with puffed sleeves, her glasses with their thick lenses, and her big feet placed her in the category of "nobody special." That scared me less than the Shetland sweater gang.

There must have been three or four of us who came up with the idea of making a best friend out of Bernadette. When you're alone all day long, it's only natural to dream of having someone with whom to walk to school, pass notes in class, spend hours on the phone, and share secrets. Having the luxury of choice, Bernadette dangled before each of us the possibility of acquiring her exclusive friendship. She flattered us all in turn, exploiting us, manipulating us one against the other with great skill.

You can't defend yourself against an unknown danger. None of us realized that we were up against a bitch.

Was it because my house was along the way to hers? I easily beat out my rivals. I was the one with whom she preferred to walk home from school. There were three bakeries along our route, and she stopped at each one to load up on chocolate teddy bears, caramels, and cream puffs, her favorite.

Since her mother had her on a diet, she ate fast, gobbling up her entire bag of sweets before she got home, but then felt guilty about eating so much candy. She'd bully me into buying some, too, so I wouldn't be watching her stuff herself all on her own.

After a month of her egging me on to buy more and more goodies, so she'd have greater plunder from my bag after emptying her own, my savings melted away like snow in the sun. For a few days I refused to give in to her demands.

One week later, when Bernadette was nowhere to be seen after school let out, I walked home alone, with a chill in my heart. Along the way, mortified, I recognized her red coat on the sidewalk across the street. She was with one of her three other suitors, and she pretended not to recognize me.

At recess the next day, she twisted the knife in the wound.

"Marion's nice, she gave me some croissants and a whole packet of caramels after school yesterday. I went to her house to do my homework."

Marion lived nowhere near Bernadette, who went by my door every day without ever wanting to stop by, in spite of my frequent invitations.

That afternoon, going home, I bought her five francs' worth of candy.

A month later, I was spending five francs a day.

This friendship was way too expensive for me, but at that price, I had the advantage over the others from then on. I had someone with whom to pass the time during recess, someone with whom to wait for the bus, someone who was finally giving me official status in the class. I wasn't the anonymous mouse anymore. I was Bernadette's best friend. That was priceless. Or to be precise, I was ready to pay the price, whatever the cost.

Every evening, I swore to myself that I wouldn't take any money to school the next day.

Every morning, the prospect of finding myself back in my corner got the better of me.

While I was getting ready to go to school one pleasant April day, I shook my piggy bank upside down over my bed. Nothing left. It was empty! I panicked. Being unable to pay for that day's bakery visits was not an option.

I absolutely had to have money.

My father was at work, my sister was in the bathroom, my mother in the kitchen. Her purse was sitting in the front hall, as usual. Why did no prohibition kick in to stop me that day? I opened her handbag, rummaged through her change purse, took a few coins. With no one the wiser. "Bye!" I shouted on my way out, unable to face my mother. I scrambled down the stairs. Those stolen coins were burning my fingers.

In a month, I swiped about one hundred and fifty francs from my mother's purse.

One evening, she almost noticed something while looking through her purse. I heard her ask my father if he'd been the one to take the twenty francs she was sure she'd put in her bag. He said no. She dumped everything out of her bag. Nothing. She went to check the pockets of her coat. I had just enough time to replace the bill in one of the change purse compartments.

It had to stop.

I managed to last four days. Four days alone in my classes, since Bernadette had suddenly forgotten my first name.

On the fifth day, I started again.

The next afternoon, when I came home from school with Bernadette, my mother was waiting for me on the sidewalk in front of our building.

Bernadette gave me a vague wave and went on home.

My mother pushed me along in front of her all the way to our living room, then shut the door.

She was shaking with anger. She demanded an explanation but didn't give me enough time to reply. In any case, there was nothing to say, understand, or explain.

The cheater who was a liar was also a thief.

I had no excuse.

What I felt had gone way beyond shame.

The stain was there and would never come out.

As with the lock of hair, I couldn't be angry at anyone. Except myself.

I looked at my mother and I felt unworthy of her, of my father, of their efforts, their sacrifices.

My mother said she was going to tell the family, so that everyone would know she had brought a worthless child into the world.

I was thinking of my grandfather. Everything I was unable to explain to my mother I said silently to him. Only he would understand that I couldn't take it anymore, always being alone at home and in school, never speaking to anyone, ever, except to Laure or to him.

As if she had read my mind, my mother abruptly grabbed my arm, forcing me to face her.

"And that's not all! I'm going to tell M. Reuter and Uncle Dee. Tell them what kind of girl my father's granddaughter turned out to be!"

That was when I decided it was time for me to go.

Life without Grandfather was tedious and sad, but if I lost my two guardian angels, there would be nothing left to keep me here. And the queen . . . What would she think of me? That I was trying to destroy our family's reputation on purpose.

And my father? Would *he*, at least, be willing to listen to me?

But he was off on a business trip until the end of the week. He hardly ever went away, maybe once a year. It was just my luck he'd left that morning.

I had no choice. I had to stop ruining their lives.

The only way to do that was to disappear.

My mother finally sent me to my "room." Through the closed dining room doors, I heard my sister come home from school and my mother whisk her off into the kitchen. I could just imagine what they were whispering. I felt sick to my stomach.

I closed the shutters, drew the drapes, unfolded the squat green armchair.

I lay down in the dark. I was shaking so much I could hear my teeth chatter.

I was inexcusable, unforgivable. Above all I was a coward, a pathetic coward. How could I have believed Bernadette would be my friend? My math teacher was right: I was way dumber than average. My family hadn't deserved this, and I . . . I no longer deserved to remain among them.

I'd hit rock bottom.

To punish myself, I did not turn on the radio before falling asleep. No oxygen for me.

The next morning, while washing up, I emptied the bottles of sleeping pills and all the other medicines Maman stores on the top shelf of the cabinet in the bathroom to keep them out of reach.

After swallowing everything, I looked in the mirror.

The mouse looked sickly.

I disgusted myself. I turned out the light so I wouldn't see me anymore.

The mouse is a louse.

Let her croak.

Part Two

I woke up in a strange room. I was alone.

There were bars on the windows.

Thin light drifted through them, but I couldn't tell whether it was dawn or dusk.

I was wearing a shift of rough material that smelled of bleach.

Throwing back the covers, I lifted up the hem to look at my stomach. No scar, no mark, nothing on my tummy or on my arms, either. I had a coated tongue, period. I'd lucked out in that department, anyway.

Nobody touched anything: that was my first thought.

My second was that I'd screwed up, since I was still there.

I sat on the bed with my back to the wall.

In front of me, a door, through which no sound filtered.

On my right, a tinplate table and chair.

On the table, a meal tray. A cellophane-wrapped plate with some ham, a plain yogurt, a packet of cookies, a piece of bread, a pat of butter, an impressively yellow apple, a spoon.

And a knife.

I leaned forward to get it. Stainless steel, lightly serrated. I tested the blade with my index finger. Poorly sharpened, but the tip was more pointed than round.

I placed the shiny knife on the white sheet and stared at it, hard.

There it was, my second chance.

If I wanted.

A slice in each wrist and presto! All done.

Still, it was funny, that knife in my room. I mean they *had* to have known why I was in there.

Outstanding negligence.

Unless it was a fateful sign.

But of what? Was the knife the sign? Or the fact that I was still alive?

Up to me to decide. When you're the target, you can't miss twice.

Not when you're alone . . . with a knife.

I hadn't asked for a second chance. I hadn't asked for anything, actually. I simply wanted to join my grandfather.

Was he behind this?

Had he arranged this for me?

A second chance.

If I had one, what would I do with it?

I'd change everything, that's for sure.

First off, I'd come out of my hole.

I'd go talk to people. To people who didn't have any queen, any Bernadette, any guardian angels. How did they do it? What kept them going?

I cannot bear being afraid anymore.

I cannot bear being alone anymore.

If my second chance is for more fear and loneliness, I choose the knife.

If not, I start again at zero.

Enough of the mouse. It's dead and gone and good riddance.

But me?

I did my best to die, I wasn't pretending, I took all the drugs, I said nothing to anyone.

How come I'm still here?

Was it an accident or my destiny?

If I stay, what am I meant to do?

If I stay, nothing stops me, I charge ahead, I do what I want.

And if that doesn't work, at least I will have tried.

Instead of hiding in my hole. Like the mouse I was.

Now I see things clearly.

Bernadette is of no importance.

My life depends on me, not on others.

Expect nothing from others; charge into the fray.

Run smack into life instead of watching it pass by.

That's what M. Reuter and Uncle Dee did. They put up a real fight.

Me, I've never fought for anything.

I bowed my head to huddle in my hole. I lived like a mouse. Basically, I did nothing.

Now I'm going to get busy.

I'm going to try.

I want to try.

~~~~~~

I was exhausted. The knife rejoined the spoon on the tray. I fell back asleep.

When I awoke, the tray was gone. But I remembered.

The knife had meant fear.

The mouse is gone.

Everything is possible.

I pressed the button on the night table. A nurse came, checked my blood pressure, and announced, "You have visitors."

My parents came into the room. I was astonished to see my father. What was he doing there? Had he returned home on my account? When I asked him, I saw his blue eyes begin to glitter; he looked so touching, trying to blink back his tears.

My mother was ashen and stared at me as if she could not get enough of me. She took my hands in hers, gripping them tightly.

I sensed that they were waiting for me to give them a sign, to put them on the right track. They were afraid of stumbling, saying the wrong thing. They needed my help.

Now they were the ones in the grip of fear.

The fear of not having seen anything coming.

The irrational fear of not knowing how to handle this new situation.

All my fear was gone. It was as if my parents had absorbed it.

That wasn't what I'd wanted.

I was the one I had tried to punish, not them.

I'd shut myself up in my hole.

If they hadn't noticed anything, it was because I'd fooled them too well.

My mind was now bathed in limpid clarity.

I was fine.

But they weren't.

So we talked about something else. Summer vacation. The mild weather. My mother had brought me my favorite cookies, she'd baked them herself.

I was out of danger, I knew that. But I didn't feel like discussing the how and why of the whole episode. Why make a fuss over my intentions at this point? Now I had all the time in the world.

I was kept at the Hôpital des Enfants-Malades for over a week. I felt good. I wasn't suffering from anything. My blood work was satisfactory.

Across the hall from me, there was a fellow "survivor." I'd learned about her through some careless remarks by the cleaning woman who came through every morning to do the floors, grumbling, "This is nutcase territory."

During those first few days, I never left my room. My mother had brought me the transistor plus some books and newspapers, but my brain was in too much of a whirl. I wasn't reading. I was housecleaning in my head. I was drawing up my battle plans.

What did I want most in the world? To work in radio. To become a journalist. Whom did I know in those professions? No one. How could I break into those fields? By learning, studying. First I would pass my baccalaureate exam. I would set to work.

I would become a good student, defying all those who had already written off my future. I would transform myself in front of everyone. I couldn't wait to begin.

After a few days, I ventured out into the corridor. The girl across the way was a pretty nineteen-year-old brunette who bit her nails and spent hours at her mirror making up her eyes and testing beauty products. She had a whole plastic bag filled with samples. She taught me what she called "the makeup rule of three," the three accessories without which no woman worthy of the name should ever leave home: powder, blush, and mascara.

Corinne was quite thin, with big green eyes. She cried a lot. She had wanted to die because of a boy who had dumped her. She talked to me about it for hours, and the more I listened to her, the more I wondered what she was doing there. Me, I'd done unforgivable things, I had real reasons to want to do away with myself. But to die for love? That seemed incredibly shallow to me.

And she, for her part, thought my story was silly.

"I mean, I steal makeup in Prisunic without batting an eye!"

Each morning at six, a nurse opened the door, turned on the light, and handed me a thermometer. On the third day, to test my new courage and fine resolutions, I dared to ask her why I had to be awakened so early when I wasn't sick.

"You're the one who got herself sent here," she replied curtly.

She felt that the presence of patients like me was an insult to the gravely ill children who shared that wing with us. In fact, she had gotten into the habit of coming to get Corinne and me at around five o'clock to help feed those children. We carried trays, we served glasses of water, we chatted with those pale patients who never left their beds.

In the evening it took me some time, in my room, to recover from their faces. And I really resented that nurse. I found it only natural to help her out and understood that it was healthy to deal head-on with misfortune. But why did she make us do it as a punishment? Did she think that was a way to make us regret what we'd done?

On the fifth day, the ward psychologist came to my room to talk to me. This short woman with her gray hair in a chignon was determined to understand why I had landed there at such a young age. To want to die at twelve years old in 1968, that didn't jibe with her statistics.

Corinne's problems didn't interest her. Broken hearts? She'd seen a raft of them. Such cases, in her opinion, were "pretend attempts." A few pills, a call for help, get your stomach pumped, and that's that.

"Whereas you," she said, leaning toward me almost greedily, "you didn't do things by halves!"

Her interest unnerved me. I didn't feel like telling her my story. I didn't need her explaining to me what I had already understood.

My attitude did not please her at all, and she informed me that she would say specifically in her report that she found my mutism symptomatic of the

autistic aspect of my personality. I wasn't impressed.
Clearly, I was feeling better and better.

Listening to a news special by Julien Besançon
on the Europe 1 station, I learned that students were
occupying the Sorbonne. I could hear the shouting even up in my room with its barred windows
overlooking the rue de Sèvres. Two weeks earlier, I
remembered, just outside my lycée, I'd been handed
a leaflet I'd thrown right into the gutter without a
glance. I'd had plenty of other things on my mind
at the time.

From then on I was glued to my transistor and
tracked the paths of the demonstrations on a map
of Paris. It was strange to follow the convulsions of
a city in turmoil on the radio, in a room in a hospi-
tal where silence reigned supreme. I felt as if I were
letting life sneak into the place like a burglar. The
nurses made me turn the sound down with reproving looks.

Corinne didn't get what was so fascinating to me
in all that. Well, I saw it as fate winking at me: while
adults were starting their revolution outside, I was
starting my own, on a personal scale. My little story
was intersecting with the big one. I was in harmony
with the world.

Back home, I found that the apartment had become too small. I had trouble accepting the familial overcrowding that had never bothered me before. I needed my own space, but I didn't want another hiding place.

So I tidied up. I threw away all my Laure notebooks, which I now saw for what they were: conclusive evidence of my mediocrity. I reviewed my class photos; I really did look like a mouse. I'd have to change my glasses and give up pigtails. I wasn't that dwarf girl anymore, but only I was aware of it. There was no outward sign of my transformation.

I returned to my piano with unexpected pleasure. Instead of sight-reading pieces and studying musical theory, I now enjoyed recreating the chords of my favorite songs. I could work for an hour until I found the perfect match for a particular harmony. In so doing, I branched out into inventing my own melodies. I tape-recorded them but wouldn't let myself listen to them until the next morning, when I would wake up with my heart pounding. *Would I think they were good?* It was an exciting way to begin the day.

I asked my mother if anyone at the lycée knew the truth. Only the principal had been told what had happened. In fact, aside from the four of us, no one else in our family knew a thing.

From the way my mother answered me, I sensed that it was out of the question for me to talk about it with anyone. She insisted that this affair had to remain a private matter. A family secret. "It's nobody else's business": that was her leitmotif.

Not tell even M. Reuter or Uncle Dee? Not them, absolutely not! My mother seemed to positively dread the idea that such information might leak out of our private circle.

I, however, wanted to spread the news to everyone, telling them how I had broken down the walls of my prison. Describing my transformation made it more concrete. I was eager to explain that the fog in which I'd gotten lost had evaporated. I longed to shout to the world that I was back among the living . . .

I did not insist. Whereas I felt I'd slammed the door on all my demons, for my parents it was different, as if they had just opened Pandora's box. My sister was still my older sibling, but the charm was broken. I had a brilliant sister. Her life no longer overshadowed mine. She was no longer my queen.

I went back to school for the last three weeks of classes. Bernadette had exchanged her coat for a polka-dotted raincoat. I met her gaze until she had to look away. I never said another word to her.

Come what may, I'll travel on
One day, and find the far horizon . . .
At last I'll find my strength and courage
And that will be my heritage . . .

"The Cavalry," a hit by the up-and-coming singer Julien Clerc, was being played and replayed on the radio, and it became the theme song of my new determination. It was a fitting accompaniment to that strange month of May. My journey had begun. There, in front of me, lay the road to my horizon.

One Wednesday morning, I walked into the office of Mme. Zouari. Still in her thirties, this woman with short brown hair, thick eyebrows, and a gruff but friendly air was sitting behind a small table cluttered with papers that she swept aside without ceremony, as if to make room for this new case she had suddenly inherited: me.

After the usual preliminaries—noting all my basic information on an index card—she said that my parents had wanted her to see me, but that she had asked them no questions. She had wanted to hear my version of events first.

Well, that was a pleasant change from the gray-haired psychologist and her statistics. Given my burning desire to tell my story, my wish was about to come true.

I let it all out. The mouse, the dwarf, my inability to talk to those closest to me, to explain that I felt myself sinking, sucked down by a bog of stifled sobs, unspoken fears, panicky dread, and massive misunderstandings. Not to mention the violation of "Thou shalt not steal" and an anguished desire to see my grandfather again, to leave an earth that was grinding me down, an earth I was dirtying with my sins and my lies.

That left the hardest part. Waking up, the knife, the second chance. My complexes, doubts, terrors, grandiose ambitions, my craving to accomplish everything that was beyond my reach.

I must have rattled on for almost an hour. When I fell silent, my head was spinning so much I took off my glasses, as if they'd had something to do with it.

Mme. Zouari was writing without giving me the slightest glance.

After a few minutes, she recapped her fountain pen and looked me in the eye.

"I think you're doing quite well," she said, with the hint of a smile. "You've performed a complete self-evaluation. There's nothing I can tell you that you don't already know."

I was dumbfounded. Finally, an adult who considered me normal! At home, they treated me like an invalid, a fragile doll, nervously watching out for anything that might tip me into a relapse.

My mother had spoken to me about four appointments between that one and summer vacation. I wondered what on earth I'd find to talk about with this woman, since she'd already understood everything.

That's when Mme. Zouari opened her appointment book and completely won my heart.

"I'm canceling the rest of our meetings. You don't need me. Now it's your parents I want to see. To explain what you hesitate to tell them."

If I'd been less shy, I would have given her a big hug.

She had just stamped my passport for a new life.

She had declared that I was right.

I have no idea how long it took me to walk home. My feet flew over the ground; my summer dress seemed to float around me. The mild air was intoxicating. What is more entrancing than Paris in June? The streets opened up before me as if I were in a musical comedy like *Les Demoiselles de Rochefort*, on a movie set in Technicolor, where I was the starring demoiselle.

I smiled at every face I saw, to share the brand-new feeling that Mme. Zouari had just inspired in me.

Joie de vivre—and an eagerness to live, the desire to live as many lives as can be crammed into a single one.

I had already wasted twelve years.

I was going to make every second count.

MICHÈLE HALBERSTADT is a journalist, author, and producer of such films as *Mr. Ibrahim*, *Farewell My Concubine*, and *Murderous Maids*, which she also cowrote. Her previous novels include *The Pianist in the Dark*, which won the Drouot Literary Prize and was short-listed for the Lilas literary prize in France.

LINDA COVERDALE has translated more than sixty books. A Chevalier de l'Ordre des Arts et des Lettres, she won the 2004 International IMPAC Dublin Literary Award, the 2006 Scott Moncrieff Prize, and the 1997 and 2008 French-American Foundation Translation Prize. She was a finalist for the 2008 French-American Foundation Translation Prize for *Life Laid Bare* (Other Press, 2007).

DEKALB
PUBLIC LIBRARY
DEKALB, IL 60115